GOD
AT THE INTERSECTION

An inspirational story of a young homeless mother's journey to change her life by letting go of the one thing holding her back, herself.

JOANIE SELLERS EDWARDS

Copyright © 2014 by Joanie Sellers Edwards

God At The Intersection
An inspirational story of a young homeless mother's journey to change her life by letting go of the one thing holding her back, herself.
by Joanie Sellers Edwards

Printed in the United States of America

ISBN 9781628714654

All rights reserved solely by the author. The author guarantees all contents are original and do not infringe upon the legal rights of any other person or work. No part of this book may be reproduced in any form without the permission of the author. The views expressed in this book are not necessarily those of the publisher.

Unless otherwise indicated, Bible quotations are taken from the New International Version (NIV). Copyright © 1973, 1978, 1984, 2011 by Biblica, Inc.™ . Used by permission. All rights reserved.

www.xulonpress.com

Dedication

To Jud- Your love means everything.
Thank you for always believing in me.

To Daddy and Lisa — Wish you were here to see the results.

To Wade, Daniel, Sadie and Lilly — Know that God is with you always.

To my mom — You are the real deal.

Thank you, Pam S., for encouraging me.

Clark F. Thank you for everything!

To God be the glory

TABLE OF CONTENTS

Dedication v

Introduction ix

1. Who We Are 13
2. The Other 10 Percent 21
3. Kim 27
4. My Mother's Eyes 37
5. All Grown Up 39
6. Five in the Morning 49
7. Stuff Just Got Real 57
8. Christmas Morning 63
9. The Cowboy 67
10. Lisa 75

11. Good-Bye to Daddy 79

12. Where We Are................................... 85

13. The Gifts 91

14. The People 93

To The Reader 97

INTRODUCTION

Ever ask yourself what would happen if you just picked up and left? You didn't tell a soul where you were going, you just left. No excuses, no looking back, no clues. One day you just couldn't stand it anymore. You knew you had to make a change, to leave the past behind, to break a bad habit and seek and find a way out. I did just that. It was five o'clock in the morning on December19, 1994. I gathered clothes, pawn-able items and two children, and I left the hopelessness behind.

That decision would prove to be biggest life-changing decision I ever made. It would change my life from that day forward, as well as the life of my children, forever. Never again would I feel hopeless, unworthy, or pitiful. My whole life up to that point had been a glass half-full mentality. Before my husband and I separated and despair set in, I had been the eternal optimist so full of Zig Ziegler, Tony Robbins, and the like. I thought sunshine radiated from my nose and that all the people in the world who felt hopeless should just talk to me. I would tell them how wonderful life was and how they shouldn't give up but just keep fighting the good fight.

My story isn't just my story. There is every reason to believe that my story is a Graham, Texas story, a banker's story, a crisis center story, a Baptist church story, car dealer's story, a realtor's story, and a cowboy's story. This is the story of an intersection in a small town where God got busy. As you read my story you will ride with me as I re-drive the same roads of my past. I pray you will have a new awareness of the single mom who struggles with the decisions she is forced to make, and that you will find a new mission in helping women in crisis or maybe your mission in life is to just pray for them. Women in crisis have hearts of gold, dreams of peace and places where they are wanted and welcomed, and hope for the future of their children.

God be with you always

My parents and me 2001

Chapter One

WHO WE ARE

I believe for the most part, people can look at their lives and determine that they are exactly who they set out to be. I read somewhere one time that we unconsciously become who we admire. Dolly Parton tells the story of her childhood and seeing a woman around her hometown of Pigeon Forge, Tennessee. She said she was captivated by the woman and her hair, make-up and clothes — so much so that she became who she thought the woman was.

Growing up in my house, there seemed to be a difference in which of us children were most like other family members. Those who knew my dad often remarked that I was "so much like him," and as I got older I began to take notice of him. He was handsome, street smart, and he was a big man. His hands were so big that he couldn't wear a wedding ring. He wasn't a heavy man, at least not when I was young. But he was a big man. He wore boots and jeans with a cowboy hat. He introduced himself much like the character in Mark Twain books, Colonel Sellers. He would shake a man's hand and say "Sellers," then add his first name, "Jesse Sellers." He looked everyone in the eye and he never interrupted anyone. He was always good-spirited. If you made him mad, you tried awfully hard, and by the time you found out how mad you made him you probably were bleeding somewhere. I was a Sellers girl. I loved being his daughter because he never, ever made me feel that I couldn't accomplish everything I set out to do, save and except hunting.

He used to tell me that I could go hunting with him when I could "pee over a ten foot pole." It took a while to figure that one out, and then one day I determined that it had nothing to do with peeing. He had other plans.

We were Southerners. My family came to Texas from North Carolina in the mid 1800s by way of Pike County, Alabama. We ate southern food, had southern ways and hospitality. My daddy was a good man who helped everyone. Money didn't assign you to his friends list. He counted everyone as friends, and the more down on your luck you were, the more he wanted to help and higher on the list you could go. Bad luck could get you a few nights on our black-and-white checkered sofa, sleeping just below the decorator wall painting of a ship lost at sea and struggling in a storm. A night or two on the black-and-white could also get you the best buttermilk biscuits and gravy you ever had.

Johnson, (my mother, whose name is not Johnson) as my dad lovingly called my mom, was the best cook in Tarrant County. No one would ever disagree with that had they ever put their feet under her table. She raised a garden every year. Fried potatoes and onions, crispy fried chicken, fried squash, and fresh sliced tomatoes was always on the menu at least one night out of the week. She canned plums and apricots, and in the winter she made sure we had buttermilk sugar biscuits. Funny thing was, with all the fat-fried meals, I was still only ninety pounds at eighteen years old.

My dad never met a stranger. He was a good listener and an even better talker. He loved country music and encouraged my singing career to a degree. Since he knew several labeled artists, he didn't exactly think I should involve myself with them because they had tendencies to use and abuse people, places and things. He was a good husband, father, brother, son and friend **90 percent of the time,** and he married his polar opposite! She was one 110 pounds soaked and wet. She was introverted and leery of strangers and their intensions. My grandmother always said she was a Caul Baby, born with a veil over her head, and she could see the future. Funny thing is, my mother is never wanted to look.

My mom was the hardest-working woman I ever knew. Till this day, I have yet to meet another woman who could spend a long summer tearing down a house piece by piece, board by board just because she didn't like the looks of it. She actually did that. She completely tore down a house to its slab and my friends and I would roller skate over that slab for the next few years.

She was a LVN student who never took the test, yet made a pretty good living caring for elderly people. She used to say she only felt sorry for children and old people.

My parent's story began in Quanah, Texas. She was seventeen and he was 19. They married, and one year and eight days later my oldest sister, who I call Keeper, was born. Then my sister Barbara, then me, and finally two years after me, my little brother Randy. They had four kids before they were twenty-three. Life was hard for two kids raising four kids and going to night school, studying truck driving and nursing, but somehow they battled his alcoholism, endured my sister Barbara's death by a drunk driver, and a marriage that was barely holding on. We lived in a little house that my mom would never sell, regardless of where we moved to for my dad's work. We had to keep coming back to that little house. It was like a safety ring that my mom just couldn't let go of.

I learned to sell like a gypsy kid learns to steal. I started at about nine years old. My dad bought and sold used equipment like dump trucks, travel trailers, and buses. My job during the week was to check the answering machine and call back all interested parties and sound knowledgeable about the item of interest. I priced the equipment, tried to sound extremely polite, and then do the take away. "We have someone coming to look at that time, could you come earlier?" We sold bird dogs, country music tour buses, and cars that wouldn't make it too far without the benefit of a few new tires and battery. My dad was always honest about what he sold and he always said, "If it falls apart, you own both pieces."

My parents picked cotton when they were kids. Like many other families, that is how they survived. Both of my grandmothers picked cotton, as did most of their children. My paternal grandfather owned a gas station and worked on cars. One time a car fell on him, and they said that he never recovered; he just kept getting sicker and sicker and died in his fifties, leaving a wife and six kids. My dad was one of two sons. He and his brother quit school to help my grandmother raise the family.

My dad was a dreamer and my mom was an oak. I always felt so blessed to be a blend of the dreamer and the voice of reason, although at times I feel conflicted. (That's a joke!) My maternal grandfather worked for Hardeman County, Texas, building roads, and he rarely liked to travel. He mostly spent his evenings watching the news and HeeHaw. He was a blue-eyed German who loved his beer. He brought his family to West Texas from Red River County. The only time he wasn't quiet was when he drank. Then he became a live wire and our mammy would try to control the current, but there was no stopping that guy. They had six children together and were married fifty-eight years.

Getting back to my mom, I guess the best way to describe her is to say that she was a tiny piece of dynamite. She and my dad together looked like Mutt and Jeff from the popular comic strip. Every day she would read her Bible and the *Fort Worth Star Telegram*. She drank from the same tea glass every day, also. She smoked Now cigarettes, but didn't inhale. Her beauty was natural, which led to her needing little makeup. The blonde hair, blue eyes, and olive complexion provided her with a natural, yet beautiful appearance. She did what my dad liked to do. She fished, drove race cars, and hunted black panthers in the deep woods of East Texas. When my father would travel the world, even working eleven months in Israel at one point, he never worried about us because she paid the bills, raised the kids, mowed the yard, and ran a very tight ship. We didn't give her too much trouble because she was a lot like John Wayne.

When my dad would drink, he became a different person, which led to her cautiously taking care of him. He would come home at 3:00am, wake up me and my sisters, and dance with us to Ray Price in the kitchen while she made him something to eat. At times, things could become unmanageable and could get ugly. The police might be called, threats would be made, and then he would leave for a few days. My dad was a binge drinker. He would binge on alcohol two, maybe three times per year. But when he did, we all suffered in different ways.

I left home when I was sixteen years old. I lived with friends, went to school, went to bars, partied, hung out with older people, and lived a fringe lifestyle. This could be a direct result of seeing a summer-filled, binge-drinking dad who ended up in rehab in Houston after being found unconscious by me. Everyone left the house when this happened. We all decided that we couldn't stay as long as he was there. This was the last big binge my dad would go on. My mom was trying to lawyer-up, and she and my little brother stayed with her boss, who was quadriplegic. My older sisters were already married and on their own, and I was running wild. I was used to being self-managed. Both my parents worked most of my life, growing up. We spent a lot of time with friends and alone.

My older sister, bless her heart, was Keeper and Reporter of all things. We were self-governed, sure, but I never forgot that she would fastidiously report any of my wrongdoings. We didn't worry too much about getting a good talking to; we were much more occupied with thoughts of belts, switches, and while it never happened, being beaten until our noses bled. The threat alone was enough to get us to bed early to make sure we made it to school on time. And The Keeper, who organized her shoes by color and seldom talked to us unless it was harsh and reprimanding, wrote pretty, cursive notes about our behavior, always lurking around corners with pad and pen in hand. The minute my folks would leave, she turned into the mean old lady from *Annie*.

I can remember her cooking for us when she was only seven years old. One time when we visited our grandparents in Quanah, she drove us all over to Oklahoma, some ten miles away, while my grandmother napped. I think Keeper was nine at the time. We sometimes went to the liquor store to buy some beer. My grandfather, who called us the Fort Worth Bandits, rode with us. We were the only ones who went to Quanah, Texas, to visit him in the summertime. I don't recall the other grandkids staying summers in Quanah.

Now, I clearly see that there were no reasons to be in Quanah at any time of the year, but particularly when it would get so hot and dry we literally watched the ground crack open and were seldom allowed inside the house during the day, as our Mammy was deeply engrossed in her soaps.

Chapter 2
THE OTHER 10 PERCENT

As I said before, my dad was a wonderful husband, father and friend *90 percent* of the time. When the thunder rolled, as it did a couple times per year, we rarely called for backup. My mother was tiny, but salty. When he chose to come into her house, disturb her children and make a mess, he was on the thinnest ice a man could walk on. The tiny tornado would give him every opportunity to see things her way, but when he bucked, she kicked. There was no stopping her, and we girls were like the Cavalry. I can't imagine how we must have looked: me climbing up one arm of the giant, the Keeper on the other, and Kim, the gymnast, hanging onto his back. We would take him down until he decided to rise up and take us with him. He never hit us; he would just kind of shake us off and say, "Alright, alright I'm leaving."

I think that was the start of my fighting spirit. I always thought we were somehow different than the rest of the world. We were protectors of the queen and we could easy defeat any enemy. We girls felt victorious because he chose to give up. We saw a white flag even if he didn't wave one. He would be gone for a few days, and then would show up again to try to make nice. We were always glad to see him because, like everyone else who knew him, we loved him. We all felt sorry for him when he came back because it seemed to be the alcohol's fault, not his. How could we stay mad when he was so wonderful the other 90 percent of the year when he didn't drink?

My dad never minded sharing with us his ideas, schemes, and plans when he wasn't binge drinking. He would cover his whole business plan with us. Once when he returned from a binge, he had been down in Mexico and came back with enough silver and turquoise to outfit a jewelry store. We all sold it for him to our friends, neighbors, and heck I may have even cold called door to door.

Alcoholism remains a baffling and powerful addiction to me. My father could have been anything at any moment, and he could build and amass a fortune and blow it all in a single drunken binge. We may have been the only people in Fort Worth, Texas who owned two old Clydesdale horses that weren't good for anything, but he won them in a card game, so we kept them. I will never forget my sophomore year of high school, while trying to be cool and smoking in the parking lot, someone looks up and says to me, "Hey who is that dude on the horse?" That dude on the horse, half-drunk and looking for his JoJo (me), was none other than my daddy. He was stopping by to see if I needed a ride home. Horseback, on Houston

Brown Shoe, a sixteen-hand quarter horse that he had bought for me and I named, he slowly strolled up to me and my smoking club. I'll never forget that day because I didn't throw my cigarette down like I normally would. The conversation as I remember went something like this:

"JoJo"

"Dad"

"You need a ride home?"

"No, Dad I don't think so, since it's 11:00 in the morning and school's not out."

"Well, you gonna stay all day?"

"Plannin' on it, and I think they kinda would like us to."

He would ride his horse downtown Fort Worth and down on the North side to the stockyards. He owned a mounted patrol security business in Fort Worth long before the Fort Worth Police were riding mounted patrol.

Later on in that summer of my sophomore year of high school, I went to the house to get some things. I found him passed out in the bathroom floor with blood all around him. I called the ambulance and he was taken to the hospital. The doctors said that he was urinating blood. He needed to sober up and quick, so they sent him to Raleigh Hills in Houston. He was gone, and I didn't know how I would get to him. I didn't have a car, much money, or any friends who could drive me that far. I just knew that I had to get there. I talked my Uncle John, who lived near Houston, into flying me in to see my dad. It took forever to get to Raleigh Hills Hospital in Houston, Texas, and I could hardly wait. One thing my Uncle John will never be accused of is speeding. At times I thought we were backtracking.

I vividly remember seeing my father lying in his hospital bed. He was not happy. He was talking to a doctor, and I was invited into the room. The only thing I remember hearing during the meeting was the doctor saying that alcoholism most often runs in families. I wanted the meeting to be over with so that I could find out if the hospital was harming him. In my sixteen-year-old mind, no good could come from a place like that. I remember him asking about all of his equipment. I gave the most recent report; then he did something that I didn't expect.

He took a cigarette package and opened it up to reveal the white paper inside. He used the white paper to write a note to Paul the banker. He wrote "Paul, my daughter will sell my equipment and sign the papers for me. Jesse Sellers."

And I did.

Who we are? We are the sum total of our own personal experiences. We are who we set out to be. I don't expect that I will ever be anything different than what I seek. I am a wife, mother, daughter, sister, friend, business woman and above all, child of God. To some I am just JoJo. That was who I was to my dad. And every success that I have must be attributed to the parents who raised me and the God who saved me.

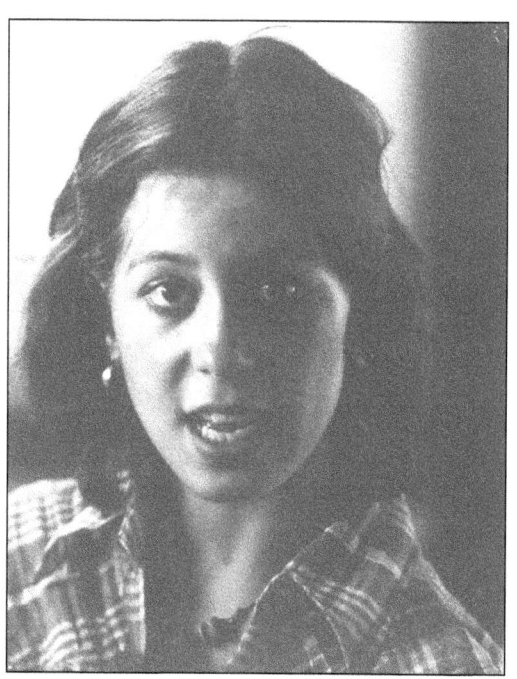

"Kim" 1979

Chapter 3

KIM

"City girls just seem to find out early, how to open doors with just a smile…" — *The Eagles*, "Lying Eyes"

Let's say that you grow up in a city the size of Fort Worth, and Dallas is your playground. You are born to two young parents who, by and large, are not that much older than you. In fact, for spits and grins, let's say you grew up with your parents. Many people have questioned this in the past and until this moment, I have never really been able to articulate how all my life experiences came to be.

We lived fast. We lived for the moment. My parents, my siblings, we did what we wanted. When my mom wanted that house torn down across the street from us, she did it by herself.

She never asked anyone for anything and wouldn't let us help because she didn't want to get us hurt.

When I wanted to sing, I sang. I found people to sing with, bars to sing in, songs to write, and never did I ask my parents if they would mind if I went to a bar at fifteen or sixteen years old to do so. I even had my fifteenth birthday party in a bar.

Even before I was driving, I was drinking and smoking. Now, none of this was sanctioned or discussed with my mother. She knew that I sang in bars, but she didn't know I was also a regular at Spencer's Palace for "10 Cent Beer Night." She knew that I dated older men, but thought that it was a phase (which it was). She prayed a lot more than she questioned, and I rarely saw her in the evenings when she wasn't reading her Bible. I think she knew that given our raising, that we would be *raising* a lot of hell. Dad was gone a lot and we, of course, behaved like innocent angels when he was home. Occasionally, he would hang cow bells on the doors to see what time we came in. We girls would flip a coin to see who would come in first and take the cow bells down. Then as we got older, he would go out early in the morning and feel the hoods of our cars to see how warm the engines still were. If we were making out in front of the house with our boyfriends, my mom would get up and come outside and knock on the car windows and say, "Your dad is getting up, get inside." That was always embarrassing for all of us.

I love my sister and my brother, and I pray for them often. We three children who are still living are not very close, but we do love one another. As siblings go, we don't share a lot of commonality. Keeper is busy with her home and grandchildren, and my brother Randy suffered a near-fatal injury, but despite the pain in a foot, he presses on doing mission work and helping anyone in need, just as my dad always had. Randy loves the Lord. I was closest to my sister, Kim, who is the second oldest. We were best friends.

My sister Kim was a pretty girl. She had big brown eyes and straight white teeth and was slender and loved to laugh. Her dark-tanned skin paired well with her golden brown hair. She was taller than Keeper and me. Being always mature, she liked to be called by her first name, Barbara.

Once, we had to move back to North Texas from a short stint in East Texas where my dad worked for HB Zachary as a crane operator. Our little house on Bird Street was rented out and we rented another house. My dad had gone to Israel to build the Three Minute Warning System with HB Zachary. He was gone eleven months. Our Saturday mornings consisted of toting laundry down the street to a Laundromat. The three of us girl were always together, and as Keeper got older, she became less obsessed with our wrongdoings and mostly focused on herself. The baskets were often too heavy for me, and I can remember my fingers hurting from the plastic squares that made up the basket.

We had not been back long when we made a new friend, named Clark. He was a hippie. He had big hair and drove a Fiat. He also owned the local Laundromat. Eventually, he would become a very influential part of my life. Clark was a talented guy who was an entrepreneur, artist, designer of sorts, and eventual architect. Being twenty-one, he was quite older than us. Kim was only thirteen at the time, and she decided that she was going to marry him.

They actually did assume a relationship, and we had to keep a secret for a while. She turned fourteen, then fifteen, then at sixteen after a huge fight with our parents that lasted months, the two parents finally gave in and allowed them to marry. She was always with him anyway, and she never wanted to be away from him, even at school. They entertained friends, traveled to artsy events, and canoed. They seemed to really be in love, but their marriage only lasted one year. It was surprising to us all, but once she was out of our parents' home and had some freedom, she wanted more. She said to me that she loved Clark, but felt the need to explore the world.

It was heartbreaking for us all because we loved Clark. He was a brother to me. He listen to me, educated me when he could, and would counsel with me when I needed help. He was a classy guy who came from the other side of the tracks, the good side. Though she never stopped loving him, that year away was a journey that no girl her age should have taken. The path was filled with drugs, bars and seedy people, and basically the wrong kind of everything.

The day before trying to get my sister and Clark back together, I had an unbelievable dream. I was in bed sound to sleep. I was dreaming about my sister and me and the airport, for some reason. I was a sound sleeper — what teenager isn't, right? I never ever before awoke for any reason, including some of the worst North Texas thunderstorms. I could sleep through anything, and everyone knew that about me, but suddenly I awoke and the feeling was overwhelming. My feet were on fire. It felt as if ants were biting me. I woke my mom and told her to get up, "Something is wrong" She asked what time it was and I glanced at the clock and it said 2:13am, and I announced it. Mother gathered up Epsom salts and a plastic pan of warm water.

After carefully examining my feet, she said to me, "Your feet are fine, I see nothing wrong, no bites, or whelps. Why don't you try to get some rest and we'll check them again in the morning?"

In the morning, I was fine. It was true. There were no signs of injury to my feet.

Kim and Clark

My sister and I had plans to meet for lunch the next day, and I planned to take her to the airport, as Clark had relocated to Tulsa. I was very excited that she would give her marriage another chance. I missed Clark, and though we spoke often, I was afraid of losing my brother forever if she didn't go back with him.

I called and called her. I thought maybe she stayed out late partying, and I just couldn't wake her up by phone. I made another call, then I sat down and I looked at my friend and I told my friend, "My sister is dead." No one told me, I just knew it. Precisely one second later, the phone rang and it was Keeper.

She screamed, "Come home, Kim's been killed!"

That was the hardest phone call to take and a hard phone call to make, as I had to be the one to tell Clark. He was crushed and so was I. He kept saying, "No, that's not true."

My heart was breaking for him, but we both had to face the facts that she was gone. There would be no reunion in Tulsa. My sister's death would be the first death in my family. The only person in my family who had passed was my paternal grandfather, who passed six years before I was born. All other grandparents, aunts, uncles, and cousins were all alive and accounted for.

My loss was great and deep. I was overcome with grief that no one could understand. I felt responsible for her death. I thought maybe I should have loaned her my car, or maybe I should have begged her to stay with me the night before. I had been praying for my sister. I knew my parents were worried about her and now we had a sober dad. He was worried about her, too. I had prayed that God would find a way to help her change her life. I thought that He had when she decided to go to Tulsa.

Before the funeral, one of my aunts, who was trying to comfort my mom, said to her, "At least you have three more children." My mom looked at her with an agony and stated, "I don't care if I had ten, I don't want to lose one."

I saw the tiny woman, who was only thirty-eight years old, question everything. I hurt for her to this day. My mother buried her daughter, who had turned eighteen years old on May 12 and was killed by a drunk driver on June 12 at 2:13am, according to the hospital. Somehow through it all, my newly sober dad did not fall off the wagon.

Kim's death had a profound impact on me, and I went dark for a year. I would look for her in old places, try to understand who she became, and punish myself for not being there with her. Once I woke up from a horrific nightmare. I dreamed that I was in the car, in the back seat as the drunk driver came barreling towards us at 100 mph. I could feel the car tumbling, glass crashing around me, and the screaming of the other person in the car. I was lying down in the backseat, bracing myself against the frame of the car, and in slow motion she turned to me from the passenger seat and said to me, "This is what happened to me."

The dream shook me to the core. It also helped me to accept that she was gone. She hadn't been a victim of a staged death. It wasn't a dream, but in fact she was dead.

I am certain that she came to me at 2:13 in the morning on June 12, 1981 as she was leaving this earth, and that was what woke me with my feet burning. She lived to be only eighteen years old for one month.

Kim - May 12 1963 to June 12, 1981

Kim and Clark

Chapter 4

MY MOTHER'S EYES

Up to this point, life had taught me to be loud, strong and free. I had not yet begun to see life through my mother's eyes. My mother was a caregiver mostly for wealthy elderly people in Fort Worth, and my mother was hard to impress. In fact, all I ever wanted to know about trashy people, my mother told me. I learned that there are different degrees of trashiness. And when you work in someone's home day in and day out, you interact with their family, you get to see some of the worst behavior and hear all of the infighting going on within the family. We had no idea wealthy people were so unhappy, wanted each other's money and often slept with neighbors, other country club members, and in-laws. And we thought we had problems....

I saw a comedy one time called *Sordid Lives*. In the movie, the son of one of the characters is talking about his issues with his therapist, and he tells about how his mom never let him believe he was a fat kid. He describes how she would buy him pants for fat kids and take the labels off of regular pants and sew them on the husky pants. She did this to help him believe that he wasn't fat. I have thought about this movie many times. My mother wouldn't let us feel sorry for ourselves, nor would she allow us to be kiss-ups. It made her angry if we were taken advantage of. She told me one time, "JoJo, you don't have to kiss anyone's ass just to get to bake in their oven." We were the underdogs and she knew it. Our level of success would depend on our view of success, and that's all that mattered to her. She saw how the other side lived and she often talked about how wonderful their lives could be if only they knew how to live it.

My mom is a hardworking, dependable worker. She is quiet and tidy. She enjoys a challenge but works best alone. A voracious reader and gardener, she enjoys being a hermit and values her privacy, so this book will definitely infringe on her somewhat. All who know her speak well of her, and if she worked for them, they held her in high regard, often thanking us for sharing her with them. She has been respected among her peers and always performed to the highest standards. She has been compensated well and even included in wills of substantial wealth. My level-headed mother, who is short on superlatives, would be my best template for my own motherhood.

Chapter 5

ALL GROWN UP

I graduated from cosmetology school at eighteen years old and finished high school at a night school program because, as you might have figured out by now, things were just a little crazy at my house. My dad's rehab and my sister's death left me far behind in school. We were getting used to our new normal; my dad was sober and we trusted it. Life became very predictable. We were two years into being normal, with no surprises, but were still tender from the death of my sister. My dad was back to buying and selling. We became the people we always intended to be. No theatrics, just a plain ole everyday family. Things were going just as it always did when my mom was in charge and my dad was on the road working. Dad would often attempt to impart wisdom to me, and it was obviously awkward at times.

The one thing that he finally said that made total sense to me was over coffee one morning, when he looked at me and said, "JoJo, don't let my mistakes, become your excuses." Those words made all the difference in the world to me, and they came at the right time. I have never forgotten them.

After graduating from cosmetology school, I was working at a salon on Fort Worth's west side. I was learning to be a stylist, but more than anything I had my eye on ownership of a salon. **And in true Sellers style, I opened my own business two months before I was twenty-one years old.** I was in college at TCJC, raising a son and married to Al, my first husband. Al was raised in the small West Texas town of Winters. He was a hell of a golfer, young and preppy with a "can do" spirit. We were both working towards higher education degrees, and eventually we moved to San Angelo where he studied nursing and I studied journalism. Every day I went in to the library to read a day-old version of the *Fort Worth Star Telegram*. My dream was to one day see my mom open the *Star* and see my name there above breaking news.

While in San Angelo we discovered we would be parents again, to a little girl we would call Lilly. After considering all options, we decided to sit out a year, go back to work, and pay for our new bundle of joy. We moved back to Fort Worth where Al would work for the Frito Lay Company.

Al and I were able to move back to West Texas, this time settling in Winters, Texas. I had decided to wait on my degree until Al had completed his degree. I had landed a pretty good gig and I was, after all, the breadwinner. I had been trained to sell "pre-need funerals," an insurance product that guaranteed the cost of the funeral if you pre-pay for it. After a while I was able to also sell caskets for a casket company out of Las Vegas. My dad always called my funeral arrangement gig, "lay away plans," which I always thought was really clever. The plan was to get Al through two more years of nursing school, and I would return to college and finish my degree in journalism. We had talked about moving back to San Angelo or even back to Fort Worth.

Within a year of settling in Winters, things began to fall apart in my marriage. I don't think it does anyone any good to go back into the archives and re-live the past. Pain is pain, and to say it was all his fault or my fault doesn't really change anything or make anything better for my kids. Suffice to say, Al and I were incompatible. No amount of time or talk would change that. We couldn't agree on anything. It didn't matter what it was, we were just miles apart. At the end of the day, no words could be spoken without harsh connotations.

On a Friday afternoon, just one day before my thirtieth birthday, Al announced that he was accepted to a med/surgery program in Austin at Seaton Medical Center. He left for Austin and I knew that it was over at that point. Even though he would come home and try to change my mind, I knew I was done. I had to leave my job and search for something closer to home so that I could care for my children. I sold a refrigerator magnet board with ads to businesses in Abilene for a small company that I started. It paid some bills but was not even close to meeting the monthly obligations. The kids and I stayed in our home until the first of December, and then I finally faced the fact that I had to move some place where I could find work. I loaded up my kids and went to Ranger, Texas, to live with my parents.

I got up every day and looked for work. I knew that if I could get closer to Fort Worth I might be able to get a better job. I set interviews, cold called businesses, car lots, cleaners, even looked at apartments and rental properties in Weatherford, just in case someone would offer a job to me.

I was reading a book at that time by Mamie McCullough, called, *I Can Bee and You Can Too*. I remember being very inspired and excited and just full of gusto, ready to turn over every stone in an effort to find gainful employment. I left early one morning, headed back to Weatherford. I decided to check the government employment route. I was told that there might be a job opening as an inspector for the county and that I should check with the judge. I went to his office, and he was very nice and understanding about how badly I wanted and needed the job. I thought I was selling myself very well, but when he finally interrupted my list of qualifications, he helped me understand that I wouldn't be a good fit for the position since it involved inspecting septic systems, and well, it was kind of a man's job. It was the end of the day and I was tired.

I spent my last few bucks on a pack of cigarettes, sat in a park, and cried.

I went home that night to my parents' house and was exhausted, sick from worrying and being disappointed. I sat in bed, writing a letter to Mamie. I explained to her that my attitude is good, my faith is strong, but my patience is running out. I never sent the letter to her, but the inspiration behind it would come in handy later on. By the time I was able to look for work again, it was two weeks before Christmas. By that time I was feeling like the lowest of the low. My parents were be very worried about how I would support my kids, find a place to live, and get my son in school, all before the beginning of the semester in January.

My whole life, I've had confidence in myself. Some people may have thought me to be arrogant or conceited, and in some cases I probably was. I had had bad experiences, and like everyone else, I defended myself. Those experiences made me stronger, but also more guarded. I don't think a person can be fully humbled unless they have identified and lost the most important thing in the world to them. To me, the most important thing in my world was the trust my children placed in me. They didn't understand why we were now living with their grandparents. They knew that their dad and I were not getting along. My son, being older, knew what divorce was about, and he was hurting deeper than he let on. I knew it but I let him keep his tough little exterior because he needed to feel strong, and it was his way of dealing with his family being so shattered. He also knew that I was trying hard to make a better place for us.

In college, I volunteered for the battered women's shelter as a fundraiser. I started a diaper challenge, a Christmas for Moms fundraiser, and did some other volunteer work within the community for disadvantaged families. I saw firsthand what battered women and children looked like, and I was pretty sure I could feel their pain and desperation. The one thing I was grateful for was that I did own a home, I wasn't a battered woman, and I had parents who wanted to help. I thanked God every day that my family was there for me. At the same time, I was concerned about the way my parents felt about me. Seeing me so weak and fragile must have been very hard for them. I was raised not to feel sorry for myself and to have a "make it happen attitude," and I am sure that I tried hard not to cry in front of them. If I had cried, they would have just sat there, quiet and not knowing what to say. Hmmm, crickets.

I wish I could have said that I was in love with my husband and I wanted him to come and make everything right, but the truth was that I had not been in love for quite some time. We had spent so much time tearing each other down and apart because we didn't trust each other to make the right decisions for the family. I hated his ideas and he hated mine. I often confided in my dad that I just didn't believe that my marriage was going to work.

He would tell me, "JoJo, not one person ever thought that your mom and I would make it. Don't give up." Over and over, I would hear this from him.

All Grown Up

I liked Al, but I didn't love him. My parents may not have liked each other from time to time, but the love was real and bound them together. To this day, I tell my children to hold on tight to love because it is the first thing to go once you begin to peel your partner apart emotionally. The layers will fall on the floor and will never float back up and wrap around that person. You can feel sorry for someone, but not enough to stay. The vision of how I saw myself in a marriage did not feel the same when I was in the marriage. It was like getting to that wonderful place you booked for vacation, then finding out when you get there that the brochure was a picture of somewhere totally different. To me, love is like a warm blanket you wrap around the person you love. You make sure that person is never without it. You never let them forget it and make certain that it never wears out and it always looks new. Al and I became necessary roommates.

Hard Lesson Cd First release

Ten years of marriage and motherhood had changed me. I was strong and loud but not free. Not the kind of free that I needed to be. I saw things much differently. I was the mother who did everything for my children. I made certain they had the benefits of sports, church, relationships, camps and family.

I wrote a song back in the early nineties that was called, "Hard Lesson." Of course it was a country song because those are the only songs I write. The song had something to do with leaving and greener grasses, but for some reason the crescendo says:

"look at all I've given up for you,
loving me the least that you can do"

Hard Lesson by
Joanie Edwards

This one still haunts me to this day. You could paint that with a broad brush, but at the time it was what a heartbreaking love song should have consisted of.

Now I would change it to say;

*"look at all I've I given up for you,
leaving me is the least that you can do"*

I think Al and I both would agree on the new ending. It was what we should have done years before. I would go on to write many more songs because it's part of who I am, but writing this story would take nineteen years. Telling the story would prove to be frightening, but I did tell it one time to strangers. I was teaching a sales training class in Houston and one of the students compared our lives. She said that for someone like myself, life looks pretty easy and I seemed to have it all together, and that life was not that great for her. She thought that I couldn't understand what it's like for some people. She described hopelessness and despair. So, in return, I began to tell my story in that small conference room to the few people I was training. It was somewhat humiliating for some reason, but as soon as I finished, I realized that I had to tell the story again and again. To keep it to myself was unfair to God, Graham, and the good people who would help me get back on my feet and change my life forever.

Chapter 6

FIVE IN THE MORNING

My parents always longed for the country life they grew up knowing. Seven years after the death of Kim, they moved to Stephens County, where my dad returned to the used car and salvage business. In December of 1994, my kids and I moved into my parents' home. If you have ever lived in someone else's home, you certainly know that feeling that you are cramping someone's style, and to pour a couple kids in the mix made the cramping a little more uncomfortable.

The holidays were upon me and I knew I had not even a dollar to spend on gifts for my kids, my parents were keeping us fed, gas was in the car and for that matter, I still had a car. I was feeling desperate and unable to sleep. I felt so badly for my parents and I wanted to go somewhere else to at the very least give them a break. I had called my sister and asked if the kids and I could come stay a couple weeks. I was hoping that a good restaurant waitress job with tips could get us in our own home really quickly. She reluctantly said yes, and I could only imagine what her new husband was thinking. She lived on the east side of Fort Worth and worked on the other side of town. She asked that I be there at a certain time, to let me in. She was a little put out, to say the least, and I began to loathe myself again. I kept telling myself how pitiful I was and how much trouble I had been already. Part of me wanted to just drive back to Winters and open back up my house. The only trouble was it was winter and there were no utilities, no groceries, and even if my parents loaned me the money again to reconnect, the next month would roll around and I would be in the same position.

I was caught in a vicious cycle. I had never been on public assistance, and I wasn't even sure if I knew how to apply for it. I didn't even know if I could qualify for help. I just knew that I was ready, willing, and able to work. And if I could find a job, all of my troubles would go away.

I got up out of bed at 4:30, and I placed the call to my sister. I then loaded up some clothes, a TV/VCR, a wedding ring, videos, and anything else I could find that I owned, into the back of my car. I grabbed some food, water, blankets, and pillows, and I made a bed in the back seat. I picked up my little baby girl, who was five at the time, and put her on one side, and my Daniel, who was nine years old, groggily climbed in the other side. As I was starting the car, my daddy turned on the light. I could see his arm up, waving for me to stop. I rolled down the window to hear him beg me not to go, but it was too late. I was leaving. I didn't even tell him where I was going, I just kept going.

I pulled into Breckenridge, Texas at 6:00am. I used the last twenty dollars to fill my tank and buy the one thing I hated most in the world, cigarettes. As my children slept in the back seat, I pulled up in front of the only pawn shop in town and began the wait for the 9:00am opening. At 9:00am, the pawnbroker showed up and opened the doors. He gave me $80 for the whole lot which included my wedding band and VCR and I got back in the car and headed down 180 East. I had not gone this way to Fort Worth before; I was only in Breckenridge to see the pawnbroker. I don't know why I didn't wait to pawn my goods in Fort Worth, as it would have been easier. Without really thinking it through, I went to Breckenridge.

I would like to say that I had my wits about me, since I was driving with two unbuckled children in the backseat, but the fact was I didn't. I had never pawned anything before and I had just sunk to a new low. I drove east knowing, that at some point I would have to turn left. The problem was I turned left way too soon. I turned left and drove some thirty miles out of the way. I didn't even remember how I got there. I was utterly shattered inside when I saw the "Welcome to Graham, Texas" sign.

My kids were stirring in the back seat. I had a whole eighty dollars to my name and now I was in a town where I knew no one. I needed a phone. I needed a friend. I needed God! I had never been so lost then or since. To say that I had a ray of hope that all would turn out fine would have been an overstatement. I didn't even have a muted or shaded ray of hope. I felt hopeless and ashamed that I had let my life get to this and now I had dragged two kids into the middle of my hopeless mess.

In most stereotypical cases, you would think that there would have been domestic abuse, drug addiction or alcoholism. I didn't have any of that. I didn't drink, use drugs or hurt people. I just could not quit sinking, and I couldn't figure out what was pulling me down. I wanted my children to have a stable home, solid foundation, and great understanding of who they are. I always saw myself as a business woman who was sort of a brass ring grabbing gambler. I just could not find a way to make a stand and burn down the bad luck and tough times that followed me. But all of that was about to change.

It was about 9:45 in the morning. I was at the intersection of Fourth Street and Elm in Graham. I was crying because my sister would be waiting to let me in and I would not be there, and I had to find a phone to call her. I was crying because I was so tired of worrying and so tired of waiting and so tired of being in control. At that point, I began to talk to God. I said to God, please take this. Please don't let Donna be angry. Please don't let my daddy cry for me. I began to tell him how I really don't even want to go back to Fort Worth. It was the last place I wanted to raise my kids. I wasn't afraid for myself. I was terrified for my kids. I knew the dangers of being a single mom in the city. I had seen the desperation in other mothers' eyes, who feared for their children. I asked God to protect my children and to keep them safe and free from danger. I told him how much I loved them and how important it was for me to start over, alone. I asked God not to be angry with me, but to help me. I humbled myself to God at the intersection of Fourth Street and Elm in Graham, Texas on December 21, 1994.

As I looked up, I saw a sign that said First Baptist Church of Graham. I looked to the right and I saw First National Bank of Graham. I eased forward, just past Everett's Jewelers and Jesse Turner's law office, and turned down Cherry Street and into the church parking lot next to the office doors. My thoughts were that if they would just let me use the phone to call my sister, that I could just kill some time until she got off work. I wouldn't even need her to meet me until then. I would be on my way, even though everything in my mind, body, and soul was telling me don't go.

The first person I saw in the First Baptist Church of Graham was a very sweet woman named Patsy. I told her that I just needed to place a long distance call to let someone know that I was on my way to Fort Worth. I explained that I was lost and that I would be on my way.

Mrs. Patsy had a warm, gentle, grandmotherly voice that could get you listening even if you didn't have the time. She explained to me that the church was searching for a new pastor and that the music director, Brother Jerry Blake, would need to approve the phone call. If I would just have a seat, she would go get Brother Jerry. I sat for a moment or two, and she asked me if I wanted coffee. I said yes.

Then I told her that my children were in the car and that I couldn't stay long. At that time, Jerry Blake appeared and asked me to follow him to his office, which was one wall away. I explained that my kids were in the car and I couldn't stay long, I just needed to make a call to Fort Worth. I told him that I would pay him for the call as soon as I could get to work, but that I only had eighty dollars in my pocket. I began to hear the voices of my children in the lobby at Mrs. Patsy's desk. It was a little alarming, because I didn't know if my kids came looking for me or if she had retrieved them. I refocused on Jerry Blake, and out of my mouth came the truth. This was a truth that I had not even heard before, and it was like God started making sense of my life.

I heard myself say, "I have had to ask for help from my parents and others. I don't like it and I don't want to do it anymore. I am a proud person, and I am smart and able to work, and I shouldn't have to ask for public help or raise my kids in an apartment in a city where I don't want to live."

Moments earlier before walking in that church, I had just humbled myself and ask God to take the wheel. He did, and He drove me to the First Baptist Church of Graham and sat me down in Jerry Blake's office to complete His mission.

The next words out of Jerry's mouth were almost enough to make me want to get back in my car and drive back to my parent's house.

He said to me, "Joanie, it is Christmas and no one is hiring anyone three days before Christmas. Do you have to make this decision today?" Those words would stay with me always: "Do you have to make this decision today?"

I said, "Yes, I have to feed my children and Christmas is here. I have no gifts and no place to live, no job.... The list goes on and on."

He told me that the church, along with other churches, had a place for women and children to stay in time of crisis. And there it was... *CRISIS*. I remembered the crisis center in San Angelo where I volunteered and helped in fundraising. I saw the black eyes, bruises, broken teeth and arm slings of many of their residents.

I couldn't expose my children to a place like that. He said that there currently were no residents. We would be the only ones there, and we could stay until after Christmas if we wanted. He asked that I at least give it a try for one night, so I committed to just that, one night.

I wouldn't notice until a few days later, but the crisis center was a stone's throw away from the intersection where God took over.

Chapter 7

STUFF JUST GOT REAL

So off we went to the Graham Area Crisis Center. We would be greeted by the executive director, Don Oldfield. Don, his wife Sharon, and his daughter Loren, lived at the center in an apartment downstairs. As we got out of the car and met Don and his family, I noticed that he had a camera. He asked to take our photo and explained that it was a state requirement. I can't imagine even now what that picture looks like. Seems like he showed it to me, but I was horrified that we were there in downtown Graham, at the former Young County Jail that had been converted to a crisis center. The building still had the hanging gallow in the middle of the structure. Once inside, I noticed that some renovations had been done. It was homier than I thought. There were nice rooms with good beds, toys, books and a large room upstairs with a kitchen and TV area.

By now, God had been in charge for about two hours. Suddenly, I realized that I didn't call my sister, but I was somehow not worried about it. It occurred to me that I was at a crisis center, and I had to focus on my children and me. In an odd sort of way, I felt liberated. Where I had felt tied in a knot, it was suddenly as if I had somehow found some air to breathe and time to think. Then Don showed us to our room. A bunk bed set for my kids and a queen bed for me. I thought then that tomorrow would be different. I still planned to go to Fort Worth. I only committed to one night. But for this particular one night, no one wanted to talk about the future. For one night, I didn't have to keep my kids in check. For one night, I could sleep. We first went into the kitchen and made lunch. Then we went into the room and took a nap. I was so tired, and I needed a few minutes to free my mind and find a way forward. I still didn't realize God had really taken control.

The next morning, we headed upstairs to the kitchen for breakfast, and as I pulled the door closed behind us, I saw a note on the door from Don. The note said, "Please come see me when you can." I was sure he wanted to discuss the checkout rules, etc. After breakfast, we went to see him, and he asked if I were planning to leave. I told him yes, and then he handed me an envelope with money. He said that some people at the church had heard about me and wanted to help. There were $150 in the envelope. I was so surprised. Don said that I now had money for Christmas. If I didn't want to leave, I didn't have to. Besides, where would I find a job two days before Christmas, anyway? He asked me to consider staying till after the holidays. I didn't know what to think. I didn't want to be a burden on anyone, especially during the holidays. Still, I didn't realize God was driving and he had the wheel.

That day was different for me. I was the self-willed, self-propelled kind of strong that didn't accept charity, didn't like to be taken care of, and I worried that someone would think badly of me for accepting charity. That was me. But all of a sudden, I was feeling differently than I ever had before. I didn't call anyone. I wasn't running from anyone. I knew that if I called my parents that Al would just stay after them till they told him where we were. I didn't want him, my parents, my friends, or anyone to know where we were. I was totally hidden. For the first time in a long time, I was letting go and I didn't even know it. I didn't know anyone so I couldn't be judged. I didn't know anyone who would make me feel ashamed for asking or receiving.

Freedom! Pure freedom! For the first time in days, I enjoyed my Daniel and Lilly. When Al and I were living together in Winters, I traveled with my job, and often I wasn't there to tuck my babies in at night. It was a deal that I had made with Al. I would work, and he would finish college. As time went on, I began to be resentful about the arrangement. I missed my kids terribly. I had not had an opportunity to spend quality time with them in months. Time free from worry and stress and hopelessness, and somehow God changed all of that. He gave me freedom. Freedom I needed to just be grateful for my children. They were smart and beautiful and didn't deserve to go through another stressful day.

The Graham Crisis Center

The Hanging Gallows

The bedroom where we lived

Chapter 8

CHRISTMAS MORNING

On Christmas morning, we awoke and went upstairs for our breakfast. Even though we had been there for a couple days, I must have been catching up on lost sleep because I don't think we woke up till late. Don came to the kitchen at breakfast to get us to come downstairs. We followed him downstairs, and much to our surprise the whole floor in the entry was covered with Christmas gifts for my children. I couldn't contain the tears, tears of gratitude, tears of hope, tears of fear that my life might always be dependent on the kindness of others. There were so many gifts that I made Daniel and Lilly choose some and leave some for the other children who might stay at the center. I never knew what churches, people or organizations to thank. There were anonymous donations taped to my door regularly. Sometimes a hundred dollars, sometimes less, but every cent was appreciated more than anyone can know.

My God had humbled me. I had called out to Him at an intersection on the corner of Fourth and Elm in Graham, and He was there. Now, I realize that He didn't come when I called, but that He was there waiting for me.

There would be many people who would answer God's call over the next several weeks. Randy and Mina were two who would come to see me at the center. They took us to dinner and signed Daniel up on a city basketball team. A local car dealer would offer me a sales position at his Ford dealership, which was the very best start a girl could get. I found a family at that dealership who would be both protective and caring. They would often check on me to make certain all was well. The owner treated me with respect and was always helpful. I never had to worry about anyone making me feel obligated in any way. I worked hard, and while it may not be the best bragging rights to boast about publicly, the owner informed years later that I still had the highest gross on record. I will always be grateful for the opportunity.

A local banker loaned me *$350 to go to Winters*, clean out my house and move our belongings to Graham.

A local real estate agent handed me a set of keys to a house she was a property manager for, telling me to pay her when I could and to just get moved in.

The First Baptist Church helped me with groceries and childcare until I was able to earn a paycheck. My first paycheck was almost $6,000.

Janie, Lilly's preschool teacher (who was also an aunt by marriage to my husband, Jud) would become our aunt. Janie was so loving and caring with Lilly. She went the extra mile to make certain that Lilly felt loved and accepted. To this day, Janie and I share a special bond and Lilly calls her an angel.

All-in-all, I think we lived at the crisis center for almost five weeks. I finally contacted my parents and let them know where I was. They were surprised to learn that I was just an hour away from them. My little brother drove over to see me, and I remember being so glad to see family. It felt like it had been months and months because so much had changed about us. My family believed that maybe I had a place to go, and they knew wherever I was that I would always put my children first, and we would be safe. My mom said that she could only pray as she always did that God was watching over us. Little did she know how true that would turn out to be. I wasn't angry with my parents, and I certainly wasn't punishing anyone. I needed space and time to consider my options. That fear of going back to Fort Worth may have been a combination of things that I experienced while growing up there. But mostly it felt unsafe and probably because my folks were no longer living there.

Jud and Joanie 1998

Chapter 9

THE COWBOY

"And all I have to offer you is what you see,
With all my faith, hope, love and honesty
So it might be hard to ask you,
To accept me as I am
And try to find forever,
In the promise of
A woman and man,
And you can't go wrong,
Can't go wrong,
Loving me."

Can't Go Wrong
By Joanie Edwards

This is a song I wrote for my husband, Jud. Just sounds like a song a used car dealer's daughter would write, huh? Can't go wrong? My buddy, Brad Sosebee, co-wrote this song with me. I wrote this song for Jud on our third wedding anniversary.

One might think that once God took control and set me on solid ground, blessing me with work, a house, and even a new car, that

I had all I could ask for. As far as I was concerned, I did. Daniel was playing basketball, my boss let me off work on Saturdays long enough to see him play, Lilly was healthy and happy, and we all were settling in quite nicely. I had to wait a bit to file for my divorce due to residency requirements, but I did file as soon as I could. Al did come and see the kids as well. I would meet his parents on a couple of occasions in the nearby town of Cisco, Texas to drop the kids off with them to visit. At the Ford dealership, I made more money than I had ever made. All was right in my world. I saw how God had worked in my life. I recognized the blessings, and I was grateful beyond words for everyone God put in my path on that December day. "To God Be The Glory."

Daniel's heart was heavy with concern for his dad. Al's visits had become somewhat infrequent. He had moved to Greenville, Texas, and worked on the road. Finding time to see his kids was difficult to do with his schedule. Al really loves his kids. It is important to note that while he and I don't agree and we have certainly had our battles, he does love his children. While Daniel was growing up, he spent time coaching him in soccer, baseball, and other activities. For a while I was a helper in Daniel's Boy Scouts pack. We both attended all things Daniel. Daniel scored highly for the gifted and talented test, which came along with its own set of challenges. I could tell that Daniel's level of interest was not what it was when he lived with his dad. It was heartbreaking, but we had to learn to overcome.

The Cowboy

Lilly on the other hand was still so little that she didn't understand the order of things anyway.

I wasn't looking for love, a co-parent, or any of the like when I settled in. There were a couple of guys who were interested, but I just could not get past where I had just been and it was much too soon to feel any kind of interest in anyone, until another fateful day near that same intersection, when I walked into Daniel's basketball practice a little late. Although I didn't think about it at the time, there was a handsome young cowboy standing in the doorway. I walked over and stood next to him and asked him for the time. He told me it was almost seven. I remember saying, "Great, what's for dinner?" I was really talking to myself, and he looked at me as if to say, "Are you flirting with me?" Instead, he responded, "I know, I have to figure that out too."

A few days later, I walked into the gym and sat next to Mina. She was asking me to take a look at a guy down on the front row sitting next to a woman. She said that he was single and that she would like for us to meet. I looked at him, but I was instantly not attracted. I told her that he reminded me of my ex-husband. After the game, Daniel and Wade Edwards, his teammate, were talking about hanging out. Daniel invited Wade to our house. We walked over to his dad and I introduced myself and realized that Wade's dad was the same guy in the doorway at practice a few days before. He looked a lot different out of his cowboy clothes. He was all dressed up for a meeting at the Emu Association, and he asked if I minded if

Sadie, his daughter, hung out too. He would pick them up in an hour or so. In about an hour, the cowboy dad shows up back at my house to retrieve his kids. Those kids would become my stepchildren some ten months later. As it turned out, Mina was actually talking about Jud, the cowboy, not the other guy who reminded me of my ex.

The handsome cowboy I met in the doorway asked me to marry him September of 1995, nine months later. We picked the kids up from school on November 16, and we marched down to the Crisis Center, where Don Oldfield married us. The road was not an easy one, and there would be some very difficult times ahead of us that would challenge us and make us wonder what God had planned. It made me question if there was another reason for my wrong turn and ending up at the intersection in the first place.

Don Oldfield, Jud and I

I had not dated anyone else in Graham other than Jud. He made me feel very good about myself. He was impressed with the struggles I had overcome. He made me feel like a hero, a survivor, like a fighter who had stumbled to his feet in the last few seconds of the fight and knocked out the opponent and took the trophy. To me, the trophy was Jud's love. The sweetest guy in the world was in love with me, and I was on top of the world and had my fighting spirit back.

Jud was born and raised in Graham, Texas. He lost the two most important men in his life in nine months, his dad and his grandfather, 1968 and 1969. His mother was an only child, but he had some extended family on his dad's side. His maternal grandmother was truly the matriarch. Jud was nine years old when his dad died. His mother would remarry a year later and take him to Stamford, Texas. Jud went kicking and screaming. It took a while to settle in. The new family would prove toxic. The only thing good to come from his nine years in Stamford was the formation of a friendship with Mark Lundgren that would last to this day. It was hard to feel lonesome when your best friend just won't let you. Jud and Mark became fast friends, spending every day together all the way to college. They did things that country boys do and shouldn't do. They would swim in rising creeks, fly airplanes, and ride bulls and anything else dangerous, just to see if they could live through it. Jud once shot himself in the hand, was snake bit in a creek, and landed a plane with a lost engine in a wheat field one hundred miles away from his landing strip on his first solo flight. He was an accomplished horsemen and cattleman at eighteen years old, running a feed and preconditioning lot and shipping cattle all over the southwest. When he was fifteen, he worked on the wheat harvest, cutting wheat as far away as Canada. And I always thought country folk were boring.

He was anything, but boring, and the one thing I love most about him is his humility. Jud never boasts about himself or tries to make himself look better than anyone else, even though he clearly could in many situations. He is self-deprecating to the extent that I feel the need to count the ways he is valuable to me and our kids. But that is part of his humility. My dad loved Jud. He often remarked that Jud was the epitome of a good man. Jud and I raised our kids together as a family, trying to be careful not to recreate the toxic environment in which he had lived in Stamford. We didn't say stepchildren, stepbrothers, stepsisters, or any of the like. We wanted our family to be whole, healthy, and happy. We tried hard to overcome the past and keep tracking forward.

Lisa

Chapter 10

LISA

If God had spoken to me and told me what I was about to get into on the fateful day at the intersection I might have spun the car around and gunned it right out of town. For those of you who think God should fill us in on his plans, you don't want to know everything God has in store for you, because if you did, you might allow the old *will* to come creeping back in and talk you out of what God has planned for you.

I was the least prepared to handle the next two years of my life with Jud's ex-wife, Lisa. There were things that I discovered later about her that would make me question why God would want me involved with her. I didn't know how to be the second wife; I didn't know how to handle mental illness; and I didn't know how to change it.

Jud's ex-wife seemed a bit crazy. She would say things about me and my children that were untrue. She created a lot of problems, even getting a copy of our medical records, and my divorce records. I could go on and on, but that would not help anything. Suffice to say, when she struggled, we all struggled.

It took years to come to terms with her suicide. It was hard for her family and hard for me. Lisa took her own life after talking with me on the phone about picking her children up from our house the following morning. I learned yet a new version of humility and finally realized later on that she wasn't crazy. She wasn't crazy at all. She was just sick and she wanted peace. I never got a chance to tell her my story of how I ended up in Graham because I was too afraid that she would use it against me somehow. I never had the chance to be her friend and not her competition, as other families have done successfully.

At Christmas, I place her picture next to my dad's picture because my dad had compassion for her. For some reason he was able to see her despair and her sadness. She was beautiful, and when the sickness didn't own her, she was very sweet and kind. She suffered from depression, migraine headaches, and a few other problems that complicated things further. I kept asking myself, after she died, what I could have done. Maybe there was nothing I could have done. She did what she thought was best for her kids. In her sick mind, she thought they would be better off. Today, I would give anything if she were here to see how beautiful and successful her children are, and to be a part of the graduations, weddings, and grandchildren.

Admittedly, I was angry with her for a long time for what she did. At one point, I even doubted that she did it. I thought maybe something sinister had happened to her. But looking back on her life as I understand it today, I can't help but wonder if all of the troubles would have dissolved had she stayed in the fight and waited on better medications and therapies. We can't know for certain, but one thing is sure, I love the children that she gave life to like my own. I feel blessed to have raised them and to have given them the love and support they've needed.

I wish no one ever had to hear the sound of children crying for a parent who has died. It is the most gut-wrenching sound. It reminded me of my intersection every time I saw the tears for the mom they loved so much. It reminded me of how I cried out to the Father to take my will at the intersection. It made me so angry and so sad. I felt helpless and unable to make them happy. I would spend the next several years trying to show them that I loved them, and at times making things worse. There can be no replacement for the parent who left so quickly. There can be no replacement, and it is hard to love someone just because they want you to. But I must say that they try, and I do too and the same can be said for Jud, Daniel and Lilly, even though Al is alive and, thankfully, well.

Jud's son, Wade, was so very strong through it all. I cried and cried and he patted me. I looked up to him one time and said, "Wade, I am so sorry, how are you? And he said, "I'm fine, but how are you?" He kept his struggles to himself, but he is a remarkable young man with a heart of gold. I am very proud of him in so many ways.

I said in the beginning that I thought of myself as an optimist that radiated sunshine. Yet, understanding the ex-wife's mental illness was far above me. I am not saying that people should not even try, but I am saying to be careful. You never know how deeply someone is hurting. I can just hear all of my words of comfort falling on the ears of someone who can't climb out of the darkness to save their life. Also, I have learned that theatrical behavior is not necessarily an act. Sometimes, it's just someone trying to change their current frame of mind. They may be trying to escape for a few minutes, and who are we to stop them?

Maybe drinking and causing chaos in our home was my dad's way of saying, "I am stressed, I miss my dad, I need leadership, I grew up too fast, I became a parent too soon, I, am not ready for this responsibility." Can you imagine the stress this must have caused my mother? She must have known that the stress drinking was a result of his fear of failure as a husband and father, and back then, it would have been very unmanly to disclose to anyone how he felt. She was the "slap him out of it" kind of gal. She was our prayer warrior, our glue that held together all that she loved. And she loved her family in her own quiet way.

Chapter 11

GOOD-BYE TO DADDY

That old dog,
Sits by the gate
Staring ahead,
Straight down the lane
He thinks you're coming back
Don't know what to do about that,

So I feed that cattle and I load the hay
Check the horses at the end of the day
Do the things that you would do
Just the way that you used to,
Before the wind, came and carried you away.
And the darkness fell
In the middle of the day,

I can almost see you ride across the sky,
Is it you
Telling me good-bye,
Ride on cowboy,
Ride on cowboy
Ride on cowboy
Cowboy ride on.

Ride On Cowboy
by Joanie Edwards (for daddy)

My folks came down to our lake house at Possum Kingdom, one sunny summer Sunday in early September 1998, to spend the day on the lake. My dad brought cast iron Dutch ovens and cooked out on the ground. He did things like that for the benefit of teaching his grandsons, Wade and Daniel, his cowboy cooking methods. He had been in the lake with the kids horsing around. It was time to check dinner that had been simmering for hours on the ground. My dad couldn't pull himself out of the water. He just couldn't get the air or strength to get on the dock.

Jud helped him, and when he got out, my mother looked at me and said, "I think something is wrong with him."

He made an appointment with our doctor in Graham, who gave him a stress test believing that maybe my father had a heart condition. Jud decided to go with him. His heart appeared to be fine and so our doctor sent him to Abilene for lung tests. I didn't worry about that. My dad had not smoked in years, and he actually hated tobacco of any kind.

His appointment in Abilene diagnosed him with pulmonary fibrosis, a death sentence. My giant was dying. I spared no horses getting a second opinion from a lung specialist in Longview, Texas. The second opinion was the same. A lung biopsy confirmed that his lungs were "honeycombed," and that he would be oxygen dependent. We were told that most people die within twenty-four months of diagnosis. But, our giant wasn't just anybody. After healing from the lung biopsy, my dad drove over to Wichita Falls, where he attended a revival. A young evangelical preacher laid hands on him and prayed, and fortunately, I would have my dad for another nine years. I thanked God every day for the extra time.

Shortly after the revival, my dad began classes to become an ordained minister for the Church of God faith. He married our son, Daniel and his wife, Krisa in 2004, and met his great-granddaughter, Kennedy. He preached three times per week up until the last six months of his life, when he began to decline. It was his time to go.

Next time I see you,
We'll be in Heaven
Heaven needs you more than we do.
And you told me not to question,
The Father,
And know that He has greater plans for you,
But oh...
I'm gonna miss you....
Oh I am gonna miss you....
Good-bye.

I'm Gonna Miss You,
by Joanie Edwards (for daddy)

I lost my daddy in January of 2008, eleven years after Lisa took her own life, and I still think of them both often. Lisa once told me that she never loved anyone except her children. I will always validate that statement for her, because I saw her struggles, and I saw her efforts. She wanted her children to be happy and healthy more than anything else.

God met me at the intersection of Fourth and Elm in Graham, Texas. He had a plan for me and for my children. He had a plan for Jud and his children. In the grand plan, He brought me to the place where I would find the most love I've ever known, learned the most valuable lessons in life, and to this day, He still amazes me. When I look into the eyes of my grandchildren, I know that they too will be recipients of the blessings I received, and we received, at the intersection of Fourth and Elm.

Christmas

Second Radio Release

Chapter 12

WHERE WE ARE

I finally did get to go to Nashville. I had songs that I had written, a small publishing company organized, a producer, and a little bit of money I raised by selling stock in my publishing company. Not long after arriving, Jud and I began to see the way of the Music Row. We were a little delusional maybe to think we could sell our songs so easily.

I made a demo and shopped it, but my plan was never to be a recording artist. I had only wanted to be a song writer, and I found that that becoming a published song writer was harder than becoming a recording artist. For one thing, we didn't want to move to Nashville. We wanted to commute just to write and wanted to be fully grounded in Texas. We did get an independent radio release, airplay, and a few very small royalty checks, but at the end of the day, Nashville is a game and if you are going to play you have to get really good at it. No one cares if you are breathing until you get a record deal. And every fifteen minutes a new hopeful gets off the bus in Nashville. The funny thing was, I heard some of the most awesome talent in places where I did my showcases, talent that I would never hear on the radio. I would listen to these artists and wonder what in the world I was doing there.

I pass by that intersection almost every time I go into Graham. Sometimes I can just see myself sitting in that Pontiac, kids in the back seat sleeping, gripping the steering wheel, with tears flowing down my red face and begging God to take my will and replace it with His will for me. I was lost, but that town and those people found me. God was there, waiting for me. I trusted Him, and He put the wheels in motion.

The story you just read chronicled my life and struggles. You were able to get up close and personal in times of my and my husband's crises. You have seen the ugly side of hopelessness and despair. The Son did shine on me and my children. Some may wonder how on earth could one woman survive and thrive while another's light went out with her own hand. I have reflected back on our circumstances many, many times. I don't want to convey that I think Lisa did the right thing by taking her life, because I don't believe that suicide is ever the right answer, and many times I wished she were here to celebrate all the successes of her children.

What I do want to convey is that since her passing there have been so many advances in mental health care, medications, and therapy. Suicide completes and ends your story, while you might be able to one day tell your story to help others. So if you ever feel that you can't take the next step, take it anyway. Reach out and reach deep within and find God. As humans, we want to control everything. We have to give our will over to God and let him lead us.

I obviously felt that if I read the right books, talked to the right people, and did the right thing every day, that sooner or later my life would be enriched. In a moment, without thinking about it, I surrendered my life to God. I just told Him to take it. My way didn't work anymore. My ability to control the outcome was diminished, and I was accountable just like an executive who made the wrong decisions and sent the company down a fast-moving elevator shaft. I just couldn't make it happen anymore. No magic words or fancy speeches would change my direction until I changed who I put my faith in. And in that moment whether I knew it or not, I was a changed woman. But I must tell you that that light that once radiated from me came back, and giving up on myself was never an option because that was all I had to hang onto, that and two children sleeping in the back seat, trusting me.

Jud's family owns one of the last great ranches on a beautiful Texas lake. The ranch has been in his family since 1937, and is situated on the northwest side of Possum Kingdom Lake in lovely Palo Pinto County, Texas. Jud had worked twenty-one years for his Uncle Ray, running his ranching and horse operation before deciding to change paths.

One afternoon, we snuck out on one of our weekend road trips, and by the time we got back, we had decided he would leave his job. We would leverage our personal assets and build a lodge on the ranch and rent out cabins to couples for weekend getaways. We cleared and burned brush for months, built seven cabins and a main lodge near the lake, and thus we opened Cedar Canyon Lodge as innkeepers. We cooked breakfast for guests using my family recipes, filled with buttermilk pancakes and biscuits with chocolate gravy. I played guitar and sang by the fire pit on Saturday nights.

The lodge did well, but it wasn't the final plan. The vision was to prove to developers that the ranch was a great location for an upscale development. All of this was able to take place in early 2001. Once the lodge was up and running, I began the process of entertaining large land developers everywhere. I called Ross Perot Jr., Ray Hunt, Centex and sometimes was able to speak directly billionaires. It worked, and within a few months, I had them all interested in our project. We were able to turn ranch land into development land and commanded a very nice price for it. It took six years to get the deal done but was worth every single day of it.

We negotiated like we had been commercial land gurus for years. I studied night and day, interviewed countless people, and we would drive or fly anywhere to gain more knowledge. There were times when we started over because deals would fall through, but never did I think it wouldn't happen. We knew that if we could gain the knowledge that it takes to understand the game that we could sell the property. I even worked in another county, selling platted lots in a subdivision just to understand land planning, entitlement, infrastructure cost, etc. Who would have ever thought that a girl like me could have pulled that off?

Forget all the reasons why it won't work and believe the one reason why it will!

Chapter 13

THE GIFTS

"For someone like yourself, life looks pretty easy and you seem to have it all together." Someone told me this some months ago as I taught a sales training class in Houston, Texas. I didn't start out this way, but I could see who I wanted to be, I could believe it, I just couldn't control it. That was up to God. God had to wait for me to give up on my way and let him take control. My will wasn't working, and when I was finally able to humble myself, I became rich in love, rich in knowledge, and rich in faith. By letting God have the one thing that was taking me down, which was my will and need to control everything, I was able to listen.

We don't always recognize the gifts God gives us. Moments after my surrender, he began to shower me with gifts. First He gave me a church. He put people in charge to make sure I got my next gift, which was The Graham Crisis Center. The next gift was a wonderful Christmas my children were able to enjoy. Soon after that He gave me the gift of employment, friendship, a home, the love of my life, my mate, my partner and best friend, Jud. Then he blessed me with two more children who would call me Mom.

Chapter 14

THE PEOPLE

It took me nineteen years to write this story. It wasn't that I didn't want to write the story, but I was fearful of it. I didn't want to look back or measure my success, because success is all subjective. I was blessed more than I could count, but I still I don't feel that my story is finished. I have so many more dreams to conquer and so many more victories to count. I don't know what complacency is because I have never allowed myself to have it. But I can tell you that I want it more than anything. I want to wake up and feel that nothing is pressing, no one is waiting on me, and there is time for everything. But the fact is, as long as God wakes me up at 3:00am, asking me to get into action, I will continue on the path I am on. There is plenty of time to sleep when I am dead, and I suppose that is my mantra.

Don't feel sorry for me, though, because I wouldn't have it any other way. I told you that my grandfather didn't like to travel, drank

Oklahoma half beer, and watched *Heehaw* every evening after work. The first time I ever heard of "sundowners," I knew exactly what it was. I could totally understand how someone could be depressed if their life consisted of work, TV, and bedtime, completely void of any kind of change in schedule or benefit of exposure to other elements in life. In fact, that exposure to my grandparents' home certainly could have been the catapult to my inability to sit still. The evenings felt dark, empty, and quiet. I didn't have the kind of grandparents who took us on vacation or planned play dates with other people's grandkids. If my sister was the keeper, they were the watchers. They watched us for my parents.

Sometimes when we are little, we are subjected to people who do not deserve praise or admiration. I discovered when I got older that for years I had adored certain people because others adored them and held them in high regard. Later on in my early twenties, I began to question why I adored some of them. I began to look at their deeds, and I wasn't trying to judge them, I was trying to find a way to commend them. As I looked deeper, I discovered many were not what I thought they were, and I could officially stop "talking them up." I could stop making them sound important to me, and it felt good to say to myself, if no one else, "I don't really like you at all!"

When I considered who was worthy of my respect, I looked at the people who helped me, and more importantly cheered me on. I didn't look to the richest, the most important, the dead or the famous. I looked to real people who had settled into life, understood the rules and had compassion for people, places, and things and other than my Mom, Dad and a few others. If it is true that we become who we admire, then you probably wonder who it is that I admire. The people of Graham who were so gracious to us are who I hope I have become like.

Mrs. Patsy and Jerry Blake at the First Baptist Church: I have thanked God for you both so many times. We are lives that you changed. God knew what he was doing when he sent us to you.

Don and Sharon Oldfield of Graham Crisis Center cradled us and made certain we felt loved.

Mina and Randy Bunyard welcomed us like long-lost friends.

Nona Jackson, you are an angel!

Del Lee, the banker with a big heart! Thanks for the loans!

Dan Sage and son, Daniel: thanks for blessing us with your book sales money.

Ray Black, thank you for the job!

There were more people, and I so wish I could know how many of you participated in our blessings. The extra money taped on the door, the toys Christmas morning, and so much more. Thank you!

Because of you, I have been able to help others as I was helped some nineteen years ago when I was the least of the least. After teaching myself to identify people I respected and understanding why I respected them, I have added hundreds more to that list, and it feels amazing to know why I love them so much.

Find out who is worthy of your respect and admiration and ask yourself why you admire them. See if you can commend them, and if you can't, find someone that you can, because they will be your influences.

At the intersection of Fourth and Elm, I was the least of the least. God was waiting to make me so much more. I want you to see my strength, but it was just as important to show you my soul and imperfections. I have defects, but He loves me perfectly.

TO THE READER

I want you to know that your life is important. God wants to enrich your life, pour blessings on you, and find you in His favor. I would also like to encourage you to discover your local crisis center. Get involved with programs that support the crisis center nearest you.

I hope you will think about Daniel, Lilly, and me and our story every Christmas, and give generously to the children staying at the crisis centers during the holidays. Make your local crisis center a priority in your giving. Some centers allow donors to adopt a room within the center.

I hope you will also think of Wade and Sadie, and be a blessing to another worthy organization, the local Suicide Prevention Center and Hotline. If we support these organizations, we help mothers who need a way out of their situation to get the help and support they need.

Your help provides a way up and way out for homeless children, children of domestic abuse, and others.

Jud and I have enjoyed success in real estate and ranching. I teach Advance Funeral Planning.

Our children are successful, adjusted, and have fulfilling lives and careers. Yes, we are blessed.

Matthew 25:35-45

New International Version (NIV)

35 For I was hungry and you gave me something to eat, I was thirsty and you gave me something to drink, I was a stranger and you invited me in, 36 I needed clothes and you clothed me, I was sick and you looked after me, I was in prison and you came to visit me.'

37 "Then the righteous will answer him, 'Lord, when did we see you hungry and feed you, or thirsty and give you something to drink? 38 When did we see you a stranger and invite you in, or needing clothes and clothe you? 39 When did we see you sick or in prison and go to visit you?'

40 "The King will reply, 'Truly I tell you, whatever you did for one of the least of these brothers and sisters of mine, you did for me.'

41 "Then he will say to those on his left, 'Depart from me, you who are cursed, into the eternal fire prepared for the devil and his angels. 42 For I was hungry and you gave me nothing to eat, I was thirsty and you gave me nothing to drink, 43 I was a stranger and you did not invite me in, I needed clothes and you did not clothe me, I was sick and in prison and you did not look after me.'

44 "They also will answer, 'Lord, when did we see you hungry or thirsty or a stranger or needing clothes or sick or in prison, and did not help you?'

45 "He will reply, 'Truly I tell you, whatever you did not do for one of the least of these, you did not do for me.'

www.ingramcontent.com/pod-product-compliance
Ingram Content Group UK Ltd.
Pitfield, Milton Keynes, MK11 3LW, UK
UKHW022222230426
12048UKWH00016BA/1013